Miss Julie *and* The Stronger

August Strindberg (1849-1912) was a Swedish dramatist, novelist, poet and essayist. His plays include *The Father* (1887), *Miss Julie* (1888), *The Stronger* (1890), *Easter* (1900), *The Dance of Death* (1900), *A Dream Play* (1902) and *The Ghost Sonata* (1907).

Frank McGuinness was born in Buncrana, Co. Donegal, and now lives in Dublin and lectures in English at University College, Dublin. His plays include *The Factory Girls* (Abbey Theatre, Dublin, 1982), *Baglady* (Abbey, 1985), *Observe the Sons of Ulster Marching Towards the Somme* (Abbey, 1985; Hampstead Theatre, London, 1986), *Innocence* (Gate Theatre, Dublin, 1986), *Carthaginians* (Abbey, 1988; Hampstead, 1989), *Mary and Lizzie* (RSC, 1989), *The Bread Man* (Gate, 1991), *Someone Who'll Watch Over Me* (Hampstead, West End and Broadway, 1992), *The Bird Sanctuary* (Abbey, 1984), *Mutabilitie* (RNT, 1997) and *Dolly West's Kitchen* (Abbey, 1999). His translations include Ibsen's *Rosmersholm* (RNT, 1987), *Peer Gynt* (Gate, 1988; RSC and international tour, 1994), *Hedda Gabler* (Roundabout Theatre, Broadway, 1994) and *A Doll's House* (Playhouse Theatre, Broadway, 1997); Chekhov's *Three Sisters* (Gate and Royal Court, 1990) and *Uncle Vanya* (Field Day Production, 1995); Lorca's *Yerma* (Abbey, 1987); Brecht's *The Threepenny Opera* (Gate, 1991), *The Caucasian Chalk Circle* (RNT, 1997); Sophocles's *Electra* (West End, Broadway, 1998); and Ostrovsky's *The Storm* (Almeida, 1998).

AUGUST STRINDBERG

Miss Julie
and
The Stronger

new versions by
Frank McGuiness

FARRAR, STRAUS AND GIROUX

NEW YORK

First published in 2000

Farrar, Strauss & Giroux
18 West 18th Street, New York 10011

Typeset by Country Setting, Kingsdown, Kent CT14 8ES

A CIP record for this book
is available from the British Library

ISBN 0-571-20543-7

MISS JULIE

from a literal translation by
Charlotte Barslund

For Julia and Tom Kilroy

Miss Julie was first co-produced by Thelma Holt and Bill Kenwright, and the West End première was at the Theatre Royal, Haymarket, on 23 February 2000, with the following cast:

Miss Julie Aisling O'Sullivan
Jean Christopher Eccleston
Kristin Maxine Peake

Directed by Michael Boyd
Designed by Tom Piper
Lighting designed by Rick Fisher

Characters

Miss Julie
Jean
Kristin

The Stage:
A large kitchen whose ceilings and side walls are hidden by drapes and borders.

The back wall stretches in up from stage left.

On the same wall there are shelves with copper, cast-iron and pewter pots.

The shelves are decorated with embossed paper.

Stage right three quarters of a large arched exit is visible with two glass doors.

Through them there is a fountain with a cupid, and flowering lilac bushes and tall upright poplars can be seen.

The corner and some of the hood of a large tiled stove can be seen stage left.

At stage right one end of the servants' white painted pine dinner table stands surrounded by some chairs.

The stove is decorated with leafy birch twigs.

The floor is strewn with juniper twigs.

On the end of the table there is a large Japanese spice jar with lilacs in bloom.

There is an ice-box, a draining board and a sink.

Above the door there is a large, old-fashioned bell, and on its left side there is a fixed speaking tube.

Frying something in a pan, Kristin stands by the stove. She wears a light coloured cotton dress and an apron. Jean enters, dressed in livery.

He carries a large pair of riding boots with spurs.

He places them somewhere visible on the floor.

Jean Off her head. The mistress. Julie. She's off her head, tonight.

Kristin So – he's here now?

Jean The Count – I took his Lordship to the station. I come back, I'm going past the barn, I walk into the dance. What do I see? Miss Julie, dancing with the gamekeeper. She's leading. Then she catches sight of me. She runs full into my arms. She asks me to dance. She starts to waltz – never seen the like of it. She's off her head.

Kristin She always was, but she's been worse the past two weeks since her engagement's been called off.

Jean What was the story there? Tell me that. He might not have had money but he had standing. People like that – if it's not one thing, it's something else. (*He sits down at the end of the table.*) I for one find it strange that a lady would rather stay at home with their servants than go off with her father to see her relatives. It's Midsummer Eve.

Kristin Maybe she can't face people after the bother with her fiancé.

Jean Maybe. But at least he was his own man. Do you know what happened, Kristin? Do you know that I saw it all – though I pretended I saw nothing.

Kristin You saw it?

Jean I did – I certainly did. The stable yard one evening, the two of them, Miss Julie putting him through his paces, that's what she called it. Do you know what happened? She had her riding whip and she made him leap over it. Like a dog. He leapt twice, and he felt the touch of the whip from her hand. Then he let her have it across the left cheek, he smashed the whip into a thousand pieces, and departed from the scene.

Kristin That's what happened, is it? No. Just as you say?

Jean That's it exactly. Now come on, Kristin, have you anything nice for me?

She takes something from the frying pan and sets the table for Jean.

Kristin A bit of kidney, that's all. I cut it off the roast veal.

Jean smells the food.

Jean Excellent. Delicious – a great *délice*. (*He touches the plate.*) You could have warmed the plate.

Kristin Listen to him – more fussy than the Count himself when he sits down to eat.

She runs her hands affectionately through his hair. He responds crossly.

Jean Don't touch me. I'm a sensitive man, you know that.

Kristin It's only because I'm mad about you and you know that.

Jean eats and Kristin opens a bottle of beer.

Jean Beer? On Midsummer Eve? I think not, thank you. I can do something better for myself. (*He opens a drawer and takes out a bottle of red wine with yellow sealing wax on the cork.*) Look – yellow sealing wax. A glass if you please. One with a stem – this you drink *pur*.

Kristin returns to the stove and puts a small pot on it.

Kristin God help the one who gets him for a husband. Such a fuss he makes.

Jean Is that so? I'd put money on you being delighted to land a strapping man like myself. I imagine you don't lose much face when people call me your intended. (*He tastes the wine.*) Good. Very good. Temperature not quite perfect though. (*He heats the glass in his hand.*)

Dijon – that's where we bought this. Without the bottle it set us back four francs a litre. There's duty on top of that. What are you cooking now? It stinks like hell.

Kristin Some dirty feed Miss Julie wants for her bitch, Diana.

Jean Kristin, would you please express yourself in a more ladylike manner? And why are you standing here sweating for that dog on Midsummer Eve? Is she not well?

Kristin She's not well. She smelt out the gamekeeper's dog. Now she has a pack of pups inside her. Miss Julie wants rid of them.

Jean Miss Julie gets on her high horse about one thing and doesn't give a tinker's curse about another. Just like her dead mother, the Countess. She was in her element in the kitchen and the barn, but she'd go nowhere with just the one horse. Her cuffs might need washing, but every button had to bear the coat of arms. As for Miss Julie, she does not give a damn about herself and her reputation. She was leaping about the barn at the dance and she tore the gamekeeper from Anna's arms, she wanted to dance with him. We'd never do a thing like that. That's what happens when the gentry demean themselves. That's when they fall. Still, she is a grand looking woman. Magnificent. The shoulder on her! And everything else.

Kristin Take it easy, will you? I know what Klara says, and she dresses her.

Jean Klara be damned. You women would eat each other out of jealousy. I've been out riding with her – and the way she dances.

Kristin Jean – will you dance with me when I'm finished?

Jean I will, of course, yes.

Kristin Is that a promise?

Jean Promise? When I say I will, then I will. The dinner was lovely, thank you.

He puts the cork in the bottle.
  Miss Julie, in the doorway, speaks offstage.

Julie I will soon return. Carry on – carry on.

Jean hides the bottle in the drawer.
  He gets up respectfully.
  Miss Julie enters and goes to Kristin at the stove.

Julie Have you finished it?

Kristin indicates Jean's presence.
  Jean asks gallantly:

Jean Are the ladies conversing in secrets?

Miss Julie hits him in the face with her handkerchief.

Julie Nosy-nosy.

Jean The beautiful smell of violets.

Miss Julie flirts back.

Julie Impudent. He knows all about perfumes too. He certainly knows how to dance. Do not peep – just go away.

Jean replies with a mixture of cheek and respect:

Jean Are the ladies brewing some witch's spell especially for Midsummer Eve? Will someone be telling fortunes? Will the stars show the man you'll marry?

Miss Julie concludes sharply:

Julie If you can see that, then you must have extra-ordinary eyesight. (*She turns to Kristin.*) Throw that in a bottle, cork it tightly. Now, Jean, come and dance with me.

Jean is reluctant.

Jean I don't wish to be disrespectful, but I promised this dance to Kristin.

Julie She can have another, can't she? What do you say, Kristin? May I borrow Jean? Will you let me?

Kristin Not for me to say. If Miss Julie lowers herself to him, he could hardly say no. Let him go. He should thank her for the honour.

Jean I honestly want to cause no offence, but I doubt if it's wise that Miss Julie should have the same partner twice in a row. People soon get the wrong notion in these cases –

Miss Julie flares up:

Julie Cases – what is he talking about? What are these notions – explain.

Jean is evasive.

Jean If Miss Julie doesn't care to follow me, then I will have to explain. It does not look well if you favour one servant above others – they might come to expect the same –

Julie Favour! The idea of it! I am shocked! I am mistress of this house. I honour the servants' dance with my presence. When I actually want to dance, I wish to do so with a partner who can lead. That way I do not look ridiculous.

Jean Miss Julie's word is my command.

Miss Julie grows gentler.

Julie Not command – don't say that. We're happy tonight – celebrating – we've stripped away all the titles.

Give me your arm, go on. Kristin, don't worry. I won't run away with your fiancé.

Jean offers her his arm and escorts Miss Julie off the stage.

PANTOMIME

This is acted as if the actress really is alone in the room. She turns her back to the audience. She doesn't look into the auditorium.

There is the faint violin music of a Scottish reel.

Kristin hums to the music as she clears up after Jean.

She washes the plate, dries it and puts it away in a cupboard.

She takes off her cook's apron.

She takes out a small mirror from a drawer in the table.

She tilts it against the jar of lilacs.

She lights a candle, heats a hairpin and curls her fringe.

She goes to the door and listens.

She returns again to the table.

She finds Miss Julie's handkerchief.

She picks it up and smells it, spreads it out pensively, smoothes it, stretches it and folds it into four parts.

Jean enters on his own.

Jean Off her head – she really is. Dancing in that manner. People standing mocking her behind the doors. Well, Kristin, what do you say to that?

Kristin She's not herself, it's her time of the month and then she's always strange. But what about yourself – will you dance with me now?

Jean I hope you're not cross because I left.

Kristin I'm not. Very little to make me cross there. I do know my place.

Jean puts his arms around her waist.

Jean Kristin, you're a sound girl and you'll make a sound wife.

Miss Julie enters, is unpleasantly surprised and remarks with forced jollity:

Julie So you have abandoned your partner – how charming.

Jean Not so, Miss Julie. I've run back to the one I left behind.

Miss Julie paces the floor.

Julie No one dances as well as you do, do you know that? Why are you wearing your uniform on Midsummer Eve? Take if off immediately.

Jean Then I must ask you, Mam, to excuse yourself – my black coat is hanging over there.

Julie Is he shy in front of me? Too shy to change a jacket? Run into your room and then toddle back. No, maybe you should stay and I won't peep.

Jean Whatever you wish, my lady.

He exits the stage right.
His arm is visible as he changes his jacket.

Julie Jean is so casual with you – is he really your fiancé?

Kristin Fiancé? He is my intended, if you like. That's what we call it.

Julie Call it?

Kristin Well, Miss Julie, yourself, had a fiancé and –

Julie That's true, but we were properly engaged –

Kristin So properly the engagement ended.

Jean enters wearing a black coat and black hat.

Julie *Très gentil, monsieur Jean, très gentil – très gentil.*

Jean *Vous voulez plaisanter, Madame.*

Julie *Et vous voulez parler français.* Where did you learn it?

Jean Switzerland. I was *sommelier* in one of the biggest hotels at Lucerne.

Julie In those clothes you look so like a gentleman. *Charmant.* (*She sits down at the table.*)

Jean You're flattering me.

Miss Julie is hurt.

Julie I'm flattering you?

Jean I'm modest by nature. That modesty prevents me from imagining that you would utter truthful compliments to one in my position, so I must take the liberty of assuming that you have exaggerated – you have indulged in flattery.

Julie Where did you learn such phraseology? You must have gone to the theatre often.

Jean I have indeed. I have been in many theatres – I have.

Julie Weren't you born here on the estate?

Jean My father worked as a labourer on the next door estate – the Attorney's. I used to see Miss Julie when she was a child, but Miss Julie did not notice me.

Julie No – is that so?

Jean Yes, that's so, I remember very clearly once – no, I can't speak about that.

Julie You can, you can, just for me. Make one exception.

Jean I can't really. Perhaps another time.

Julie Another time may never arrive. What's the danger in telling me now?

Jean No danger – I just don't want to. Look at that one.

He points to Kristin who has fallen asleep in a chair by the stove.

Julie That one will make the most divine wife – she will. Does she snore as well, perhaps?

Jean She doesn't – she does talk in her sleep though.

Miss Julie asks cynically:

Julie She talks in her sleep – how do you know?

He replies cheekily:

Jean I've heard her.

There is a pause and they watch each other.

Julie Sit down – won't you?

Jean In your presence I am now allowed to sit?

Julie If I command you?

Jean I'll obey.

Julie Sit down – no, wait. Fetch me something to drink first.

Jean I don't know if we have anything cold. Beer – that's all – I think.

Julie That's all right. I have simple tastes. Beer suits me more than wine.

He takes a bottle of beer from the ice-box.
He looks in the cupboard for a glass and plate.
He serves her.

Thank you. Have one yourself – go on.

Jean I'm not a beer man. But if Miss Julie commands –

Julie Commands? My good sir, I believe it is manners to keep your lady company.

Jean That is absolutely true. (*He opens another bottle and takes a glass.*)

Julie Now – drink a toast to me.

He hesitates.

I do believe the poor boy is shy.

On his knees, parodying, he raises his glass.

Jean Oh mistress mine!

Julie Bravo! Kiss my shoe – now – you have to – then it is finished.

He hesitates, but then grasps her foot gamely and kisses it lightly.

Excellent. You should have been an actor.

He gets up.

Jean This is not right, Miss Julie. What if someone came in and saw us –

Julie What if?

Jean People gossip. That's what if. If Miss Julie knew how their tongues were wagging up there just now –

Julie What were they saying? Talking about me? Sit down.

He sits down.

Jean I don't want to insult you – there were statements made that cast aspersions of the kind that – you know yourself. You're not a child. They see a lady on her own drinking at night with a man, even a servant, then –

Julie What then? Anyway, we're not on our own. Kristin, she's here.

Jean She's dead to the world.

She rises.

Julie Kristin? Are you sleeping?

Kristin mumbles in her sleep.

Kristin? She has a gift for this. Sleeping.

Kristin mutters in her sleep.

Kristin Boots – polish the Count's – coffee – hurry – make coffee – hurry.

Miss Julie grabs Kristin's nose.

Julie Wake up.

Jean answers her sternly:

Jean Don't disturb her sleep.

Miss Julie reacts sharply:

Julie What?

Jean A woman slaving over a stove all day has the right to be tired at night-time. You should respect the sleep –

Miss Julie is pacing the floor.

Julie A beautiful thought – it does him great credit. Thank you. (*She offers him her hand.*) Now gather some lilacs with me.

Jean With Miss Julie?

Julie Me!

Jean That is not right. Absolutely not.

Julie I don't follow your way of thinking. Have you imagined something and you believe it?

Jean I don't, but the servants will –

Julie Believe I'm in love with a servant?

Jean I'm not an arrogant man, but there have been cases, and the servants will say anything. Nothing is sacred.

Julie I do believe the man's an aristocrat.

Jean I am. Yes.

Julie I demean myself –

Jean Miss Julie, don't demean yourself. Listen to me. Not a living soul will believe you did it by choice. People will swear that you fell.

Julie I think more of people than you do. Go on – come on. (*She looks at him pleadingly.*)

Jean You're a strange being – do you know that?

Julie Am I? Are you? Yes. Everything is strange. Life itself. All of us. Everything. A mess, tossing and turning across the water and then it sinks – it sinks. I'm suddenly thinking of a dream I always have. I'm on top of a pillar. I've climbed up here, and I see no way of getting down, but I do not have the courage to throw myself. I want so much to fall, but I don't fall, and I'll have no peace until I come down, no rest until down I come, down to the field. And when I reach the field, I want to walk into the earth. Have you ever felt anything like that?

Jean No. When I dream, I'm lying beneath a big tree in a deep forest. I want to get up, right up to the top, I want to be able to see where the sun shines bright over the whole countryside. I want to rob the bird's nest and steal the golden eggs. I climb and I climb, but the tree trunk is thick, it's slippery, and the first branch is so far away. I do know that if I could only reach that first branch, then I could climb to the top – like stepping up a ladder. I've not reached it yet, I can't, but I will, even if I'm only dreaming.

Julie I'm standing talking to you about dreams – come on. To the fields.

She offers him her arm and they move to go.

Jean If we step on top of nine flowers tonight, Miss Julie, then our dreams will come true this Midsummer Night.

They go to the doorway.
Jean puts one hand up to his eye.

Julie What have you got in your eye? Let me see.

Jean Nothing. Just dirt. It'll pass.

Julie My dress – the sleeve has scratched you. Sit down, I'll help you.

She takes his arm and sits him down.
She clasps his head and pulls it backwards.
With the corner of her handkerchief she tries to clean his eye.

Sit still. Absolutely still. (*She slaps his hand.*) Do as I tell you. Now – now – a big strong boy – (*She feels his upper arm.*) Such strength.

Jean warns her:

Jean Miss Julie –

Kristin wakes up and walks sleepily off stage right to lie down.

Julie Yes, monsieur Jean.

Jean *Attention. Je ne suis qu'un homme.*

Julie Sit still. Listen to me. Say thank you, kiss my hand.

Jean Miss Julie, listen to me. Kristin has gone to lie down. Listen to me – will you?

Julie First kiss my hand.

Jean Listen to me.

Julie First kiss my hand.

Jean Yes, but on your own head be it.

Julie Be what?

Jean You're twenty-five – are you still a child? Do you not know you can be burnt playing with fire?

Julie Not me – I'm insured.

Jean You are not – no. Even if you are, there is still dangerous fire around here.

Julie Are you referring to yourself?

Jean I am. I am a young man –

Julie Of beautiful appearance. What arrogance. Beyond belief. You are Don Juan, perhaps. Or Joseph. My God, I believe he is a Joseph.

Jean You believe that.

Julie I'm half frightened.

*Jean tries to put his arms around her and kiss her.
She slaps him across the face.*

Julie No.

Jean Are you playing or are you serious?

Julie Serious.

Jean You always are – even when you're playing. That's what's dangerous. Now I'm tired of playing. Give me permission to return to my work. The Count will need his boots on time, and it's well after midnight.

Julie Put the boots away.

Jean No. That's my job – I do it well, that's my duty. I've never imagined myself as your playmate, I never will be, I think too much of myself to be that.

Julie Proud, aren't you?

Jean Sometimes I am, other times I'm not.

Julie Have you ever known love?

Jean We don't say that word. There's been girls I like. One time I couldn't get the girl I wanted, and I was sick. I couldn't eat, I couldn't drink for love, just like the princes in the Arabian Nights.

Julie Who was she?

Jean is silent.

Who was she?

Jean You can't make me tell you that.

Julie If I ask you as a friend – an equal – who was she?

Jean You.

Miss Julie sits down.

Julie How entertaining.

Jean If you like, yes. Ridiculous. That was the story I couldn't tell you before. I will now. Do you know what the world looks like from down here – no, you don't. You're like the hawk and the falcon. They fly so high above you rarely see their backs. I lived in a hovel on the estate. Seven brothers and sisters – a pig as well – in a dirty field where there wasn't a tree growing. From the window though, I could see the wall around the Count's park, and the orchard of apples rising above it. It was the Garden of Eden. And standing guard there were multitudes of evil angels with their swords on fire. But still I was like the other lads – I discovered the way to the tree of life – you despise me now –

Julie Do I? All boys thieve apples.

Jean You say that now, but you still despise me. It doesn't matter. I went with my mother one day into the vegetable garden to weed the onion beds. There was a Turkish pavilion beside the garden. Jasmine trees shaded it, the honeysuckle drowned it. I didn't know what it was for but I'd never set eyes before on such a beautiful building. People went in and out again, and one day the door was left open. I sneaked in, I saw the wall covered with pictures, kings and emperors. Red curtains with tassels covered the windows. Do you know where I was now – you do – I – (*He picks a lilac flower and holds it under Miss Julie's nose.*) I'd never been inside a big house – never seen anything but the church, but this was more lovely. No matter where my thoughts wandered, they always came back to – that. Bit by bit the desire was eating me that one day I would enjoy the pleasure of – . *Enfin*, I did sneak in, I saw and wondered. Then somebody came in, in to the beautiful pavilion. There was one exit for the gentry out of there. For my kind there was another. I had to climb through that stinking pit – no choice in it.

Miss Julie has taken the lilac and let it drop on to the table.

I leapt out and I ran through the raspberries, all across the strawberries and I finished up on the rose terrace. I could see a pink dress there – a pair of white stockings. It was you. I crawled under a pile of weeds. Imagine me hiding under thistles prickling me, all damp and soiled and stinking. I watched you walk among the roses. I thought that if it's true a thief can get into Heaven and live among the angels, then it's strange that the child of a man who labours on God's earth can't enter the park and play with the Count's daughter.

Miss Julie asks painfully:

Julie Wouldn't all poor children think the same thing as you did if they were where you were?

Jean hesitates at first, then is convinced.

Jean All poor – they would – yes – of course.

Julie Poverty must be awful.

In deep pain, Jean is very moved.

Jean Miss Julie – Miss Julie. A dog might lie on the Countess's sofa, a lady's hand might caress a horse's nose, but a poor child – (*He walks.*) A man might pull himself up by his own boot laces, if he has it in him. So they say, but how often does that happen? So, do you know what I did? I waded into the stream with my clothes on. Hauled out and beaten blue. The next Sunday, my father and the rest of the house had gone off to my grandmother's, I arranged that I could stay

at home. I washed myself with warm water and soap.
I donned my Sunday best and went to church where
I would see you. I did see you and I went home wanting
to die – going to die. I wanted to do it beautifully – in
complete comfort, with no pain. I remembered then it
was dangerous to sleep under an elder bush. We had
one which was just bursting into bloom. I ripped all
its flowers from it and I made a bed in the oat bin. Oats
are so smooth – have you noticed? They touch like skin,
human soft – anyway, I slammed the lid shut and nodded
off. I fell asleep and woke up a very sick boy. But as you
can see, I did not die. What was I doing? Don't ask me.
I had no hope of winning. You were a sign that I should
abandon hope of ever rising from the class I was born
into.

Julie You know, you have a charming way with words.
Did you go to school?

Jean A short while. I have read a lot of novels and I've
gone to the theatre. I've heard the gentry talking as
well – that's where I learned the most.

Julie You stand there listening to us speak, do you?

Jean I do. And I've heard plenty, let me tell you, when
I'm sitting on the coachman's seat or rowing the boat.
I once heard Miss Julie and a lady friend –

Julie Did you – what did you hear?

Jean That would be telling, wouldn't it? I did raise my
eyebrows a little – where did you learn those words?
That I couldn't understand. Maybe deep down there is
not such a difference between us all as people think.

Julie How dare you. We don't behave the way you do
when we're engaged.

Jean fixes her with his eyes.

25

Jean You're sure? Miss Julie, please don't act the innocent –

Julie I gave my love to a good-for-nothing.

Jean Women always say that – afterwards.

Julie Always?

Jean I'd say always. I've heard it said so many times in so many different cases.

Julie What cases?

Jean This one for instance. The last time –

Julie Stop. I don't want to hear any more.

Jean She didn't either. Very strange. So I ask your permission to go to bed.

She answers softly:

Julie Go to bed? On Midsummer Eve?

Jean Yes. I'm not in the mood for leaping about with the herd up there.

Julie Get the key to the boat and row me out on the lake. I want to see the sun rise.

Jean Is that wise?

Julie Are you worried about my reputation?

Jean Why shouldn't I be? I'd prefer not to be taken for a fool. I'd prefer not to be sacked without a reference now that I'm starting to stand on my own two feet. And I think I have a certain obligation to Kristin.

Julie I understand – it's Kristin now –

Jean It's you as well. Take my advice, go upstairs and go to bed.

Julie Am I to do as you command?

Jean Yes, for once – for your own sake. I'm begging you. Night's falling. Tiredness is like drink, it makes your head light. Go to bed. If I'm not mistaken, I can hear people coming to look for me. If they find the two of us, you have had it.

The crowd's voices are heard singing.

Voices
   A lady she walked by the shore
   She was wanting to wash her feet
   She was looking for sailors and more
   And a handsome young man she did meet

   Will you lie down with me on the sand
   And I'll take you from here to Peru
   I'll kiss more than your lily white hand
   I'll leave your dainty cheek black and blue

   The lady she laid on her back
   Her petticoats sheets in the wind
   The bucko he emptied his sack
   And they called it original sin

   Will you lie down with me on the sand
   And I'll take you from here to Peru
   I'll kiss more than your lily white hand
   I'll leave your dainty cheek black and blue

   A lady she walked by the shore
   She was wanting to wash her feet
   She was looking for sailors and more
   And a handsome young man she did meet

Julie I know my servants. I love them the way they love me. You'll see. Let them come.

Jean They do not love you, Miss Julie. They eat your food, and afterwards they spit at you. Believe me. Listen to them. Listen to the words they are singing. No, don't listen.

She listens.

Julie What are they singing?

Jean A dirty song. About you and me.

Julie Damn them – they're filth –

Jean A pack of cowards. When you're in that kind of fight, you can only run –

Julie Run where? We can't get out. We can't go in to Kristin.

Jean We can't. My room? We have to. And you can trust me. I am your friend – a genuine friend.

Julie What if – what if they look in there?

Jean I'll bolt the door. If they break it down, I'll shoot. Come on. (*He gets on his knees.*) Come on.

Miss Julie asks urgently:

Julie Promise me –

Jean I swear.

DANCE

Peasants enter in their best clothes, with flowers in their hats, led by a fiddler.
A keg of beer and a bottle of schnapps, decorated with leaves, are placed on the table.
Glasses are found.
They drink.
They form a circle and dance, singing 'A Lady She Walked by the Shore'.
When this is over, they exit, singing.

Miss Julie enters on her own.
  She sees the mess in the kitchen and clasps her hands.
  She takes a powder puff and powders her face.
  Jean enters, excited.

Jean You saw that – you heard it. Do you think we can stay here?

Julie We can't, no. What are we going to do?

Jean Leave, go abroad, far away.

Julie Go abroad? All right – where?

Jean Switzerland, or the Italian Lakes – you've never been there?

Julie No. Is it beautiful there?

Jean The summer lasts for ever. Orange trees and laurels.

Julie How will we live there?

Jean I'll open a hotel – first-class service, first-class guests.

Julie A hotel?

Jean Believe me, that's the way to live. New people all the time, new language. There's no such thing as an idle minute to complain or to worry. Always something to do – endless work. The bell rings night and day. The train whistles. The carriages coming and going. And the gold piles in. That's the life.

Julie Yes, that's living. And me –

Jean The mistress of the house. The hotel's pride and joy. You have looks, you have style – it has to be a success, it's bound to. Mighty. You'll rule like a queen behind the counter – you'll press an electric bell and the slaves will come running. The guests file past your throne and lay their gifts upon your table – you'll terrify them. You won't believe how it puts the wind up people to be presented with a bill. I'll salt the bills and you'll sugar them with your sweetest smile. We'll get away from this place. (*He takes a timetable from his pocket.*) The next train, now. We'll hit Malmö by six-thirty, Hamburg tomorrow morning, eight-forty. Frankfurt – Basle – a day later through the St Gothard Pass into Como, let me see, in three days. Three days.

Julie This is all grand, but Jean, give me courage – you must. Tell me you love me. Put your arms about me.

He hesitates.

Jean I want to – but I daren't. Not in this house again. I have no doubt – I love you – can you doubt that, Miss Julie?

She answers shyly, very womanly:

Julie Julie. Call me Julie. We're equals now. Julie.

He is tormented.

Jean I can't. We are not equals as long as we're standing in this house. The past is between us, there's the Count. I respect him more than any other I've ever met. If I see his gloves lying on a chair it's enough to make me a small child. If I hear the bell ringing I leap like a frightened horse. I can see him, boots standing there, so straight and proud, and I can feel my back bending. (*He kicks the boots.*) Old woman's talk – bigotry – we drank it in our mother's milk and it's as easy to spew out. We'll go to another country – a republic – they will grovel before me in my servant's uniform. They can grovel, I won't. I wasn't born to do that. I have something in me. I have a man's nature. If I can only grab that first branch, then watch me climb. I might be a servant today, but next year I'll own a hotel. In ten years' time I'll be living off my money. I'll travel then to Romania and get myself a decoration. I may – note that I say may – just end up a Count.

Julie Good, excellent.

Jean In Romania you can buy a Count's title and then I'll make you a Countess after all. My Countess.

Julie I'm leaving all that behind me. I care nothing about that. Say you love me. If you don't – yes, if you don't – what am I?

Jean I'll say it till it's coming out your ears – just wait – but not here, not here. Above all else show no feelings in this place, or we'll be lost. We have to look at things with a cold eye. Behave like logical people.

He takes out a cigar, cuts it and lights it.

You sit there – I'll sit here – we'll talk as if nothing happened.

Julie God almighty, have you no feelings?

Jean Feelings? I am the most passionate man, but I can control myself.

Julie You kissed my shoe a minute ago – and now –

Jean That was then – now we've other things to talk about.

Julie Don't speak so roughly to me.

Jean I'm speaking wisely. We've made one foolish mistake, we're not making another. The Count could walk in at any minute and before that happens we have to decide what's to be our destiny. What do you make of my plans for our future – do you approve?

Julie They seem sensible enough, but I do have one question. Such a big undertaking is going to need a lot of capital. Do you have any?

He chews on his cigar.

Jean Me? I certainly do. I'm an expert in my field, I have enormous experience. I'm fluent in many languages. That's what I call capital.

Julie But it won't buy you a railway ticket.

Jean Very true – that's why I'm looking for a partner who can provide the funds.

Julie Where are you going to find one at such short notice?

Jean That's your job if you want to come with me.

Julie I can't do that, I own nothing myself.

There is a pause.

Jean Then that's that –

Julie So.

Jean Things stay as they are.

Julie Do you think I'll live in this house as your whore? Do you think I'll let people point the finger at me? Do you think I can look my father in the face after this? No. Get me away from this place. I am humiliated – I am disgraced. Christ, what have I done – Christ – (*She sobs.*)

Jean Please don't start on that same old song. What have you done? The same as many have done before you.

She screams convulsively.

Julie You take me now. I've fallen – I'm falling –

Jean Fall down to my level and I'll lift you up again.

Julie What power drove me to you? The terror of the weak before the strong? As I fall, you rise – is that it? Or was it love? Is this love? Do you know what love is?

Jean I'd say I do, yes. Do you think I've not done it before?

Julie The way you speak and the way you think –

Jean It's what I learned, it's what I'm like. Don't act the lady – we're two peas in the pod now. That's right, girl, come on and I'll feed you a drink. (*He opens the drawer in the table and takes out the wine bottle. He fills up two used wine glasses.*)

Julie That wine – where did you get it?

Jean The cellar.

Julie My father's burgundy.

Jean Isn't it good enough for his son-in-law?

Julie And I was drinking beer – me –

Jean Just goes to show you have poorer taste than myself.

Julie Thief.

Jean Are you going to tell Daddy?

Julie Jesus, have I been aiding and abetting a thief? Have I been drunk or dreaming this Midsummer Night? A night of innocent games –

Jean Innocent my arse.

She paces up and down the room.

Julie Am I the most unfortunate alive on this earth?

Jean Why are you unfortunate? Look what you've won. Think of Kristin in there. Maybe you don't believe she has feelings as well.

Julie I did think so once. Not now. A servant is a servant –

Jean And a whore is a whore.

She is on her knees with her hands clasped.

Julie God above, end my life. Save me from the filth I've fallen into. Save me – please.

Jean I must admit I am sorry for you. When I was hiding in the onion beds watching you in the rose garden you must know I was entertaining the same dirty thoughts every other boy thinks.

Julie You said you would die for me.

Jean In the oat bin? Talking rubbish.

Julie You were lying?

Jean begins to grow sleepy.

Jean I suppose I was. I think I read the story in some newspaper – a chimney sweep lay down in a box of lilacs – he'd been ordered to pay child maintenance –

Julie And that's your like, is it?

Jean I had to think of something. Women fall for fancy stories.

Julie Pig.

Jean *Merde.*

Julie Now you've seen the hawk on its back –

Jean Not quite on its back –

Julie And I was to be the first branch –

Jean But the branch was rotten –

Julie I was to be the sign above the hotel –

Jean And I was to be the hotel –

Julie Trapped behind your counter, tempting the guests, cheating on the bills –

Jean I would do that myself –

Julie Could a human being sink so low in the dirt?

Jean Then clean it.

Julie Servant – lackey – get to your feet when I speak.

Jean Servant's whore – lackey's lick – shut up and get out. You stand here telling me that I'm filth? None of my kind has acted the filthy way you did tonight. Do you think any serving girl would throw herself at a man the way you did? Have you ever seen a girl from my class hand herself over like that? I've seen it with animals, I've seen it with whores. Oh, I know your class lets it happen. What do they call it? Being liberated. Emancipated – something fancy like that. Yes, I've seen great ladies wag their arses at soldiers and waiters.

She is crushed.

Julie That's right. Hit me. Walk on me. I deserve no better. I'm an unfortunate woman – so help me. Show me how to get out of this if you know a way.

He speaks more gently.

Jean I won't deny my share in the honour of seducing you – that would be shaming myself. But do you really believe a man in my position would have dared to look at you unless you offered the invitation yourself? I am still amazed –

Julie And are you proud of it –

Jean Why should I not be? I do admit though that I won too easily to give me complete pleasure.

Julie Go on – hit me again.

He gets up.

35

Jean No – forgive what I have just said. I wouldn't hit a defenceless man, let alone a woman. Yes, it's good to learn that you blinded us beneath you with fool's gold – the hawk's back was not too fine, the porcelain cheeks were powdered and the elegant nails had black beneath them. The handkerchief may smell of perfume but it's soiled. Still, it hurts me to know that what I wanted amounted to so little, so very, very little. It hurts me to see you fall so low that you're far beneath your cook. It hurts me the way flowers in the harvest are washed away by the rain and churned into dirt.

Julie You're talking as if you're already looking down on me.

Jean I do – I do. You see, I could make you a Countess, but you can never turn me into a Count.

Julie But I'm still the child of a Count, and you can never be that.

Jean True, but I could father Counts if –

Julie You thieve – I don't.

Jean Thieving's not that bad. There's worse you could learn to do. By the way, as a servant of this establishment I count myself to some extent a part of the family. A child of the house, you might say. It's not really thieving when the child grabs a berry from the branches that are full. (*His passion is aroused once more.*) Miss Julie, you are an extraordinary woman. Far too good for my like. You were drunk, you made a mistake, and you want to cover that up by believing that you're in love with me. You are not – maybe you fancy my fine features – and so your love's no better than mine. Me though, I'd hate to be your animal, and I can never win your heart.

Julie Are you sure about that?

Jean You're going to say that I can. I should be able to love you absolutely. You are beautiful, and wealthy – (*He moves closer to her and takes her hand.*) Clever, kind when you choose to be, and when you have a man on fire, those flames will never die.

He puts his arms around her waist.

You're a strong wine – warm – the smell is powerful – and to kiss you –

He attempts to lead her offstage, but she quickly frees herself.

Julie Get your hands off me. You won't win me like that – no.

Jean How then? No sweet nothings – not like that – no caresses? Not by planning the future, saving you from disgrace – how do I win you?

Julie How? I don't know how. I do not know. I hate you the way I hate a rat, but I can't get away from you.

Jean Escape with me.

She straightens up.

Julie Escape – we'll escape, yes. I am tired out. Get me a glass of wine.

Jean pours the wine.
Miss Julie looks at her watch.

Julie We have to talk first – we have a bit of time – (*She empties her glass and holds it out for more.*)

Jean Stop drinking so much – you'll get drunk.

Julie Who cares?

Jean Who cares? It's bad manners to get drunk. What were you going to say to me?

37

Julie We must escape. But first of all we need to talk – I mean I need to talk. So far you've done all the talking. You've told me about your life. I want to tell you now about mine. Before we begin our journey, we have to know each other completely.

Jean Hold on. Make sure you won't regret spilling out your life's secrets.

Julie Are you not my friend?

Jean Sometimes I am, but don't count on me.

Julie You don't mean that. Anyway, my secrets are everybody's business. My mother had no noble blood. She came from very ordinary stock. She was reared in the ideas of her time – woman's emancipation, equality, all that sort of thing. And she loathed marriage. When my father proposed, she said she could never be his wife, but he could be her lover. He told her he didn't wish the woman he loved to receive less respect than he himself would. She told him that such things meant nothing to her, and being madly in love he agreed to her terms. From that day on his own kind didn't recognise him. This imprisoned him in family life, and that did not satisfy him. I was born and, as far as I can understand it, my mother did not want that. My mother wanted to rear me as a child of nature. I also had to learn everything a boy is taught. I was to become an example of how a woman could be just as good as a man. I wore boy's clothes. I was taught to tame horses, but never to milk in the barn. I had to groom and harness. I had to learn about farming – hunting – even slaughtering. It was frightening. Throughout the estate men were ordered to do women's work, and the women to do men's. So, the estate fell to ruin. We were the laughing stock of the whole neighbourhood. My father must have finally come out from under his spell. He turned against it all and everything was changed to the way he wanted it. My parents were soon married quietly. My mother took ill – I don't know from what – she hid in the garden – some nights she stayed outside. You've heard about the big fire – that came next. The house, the stable, the barn – all burned down in mysterious circumstances. It was probably an act of arson, because the catastrophe happened the day after the quarterly insurance had run out. My father had sent the renewal premium, but it was delayed – the servant carrying it was careless – and it didn't arrive on time. (*She fills the glass and drinks wine.*)

Jean Don't drink any more.

Julie Who cares? We were left with the clothes we stood in. We had to sleep in the carriages. My father had neglected most of his old friends. They had forgotten him completely. He didn't know where to get money to build the house up again. My mother remembered a friend from her youth. A brickmaker – he lived near here. My mother urged my father to borrow from this man. He did borrow and he was not allowed to pay a penny interest. That astonished him. So the house rose again from the ashes. (*She drinks again.*) Do you know who burned down the house?

Jean Your most exalted mother?

Julie Do you know who the brickmaker was?

Jean Your mother's lover.

Julie Do you know whose money it was?

Jean Hold on – I don't know – whose?

Julie My mother's.

Jean Then it was the Count's as well, unless they made a marriage settlement.

Julie There was no settlement. My mother had a small fortune. She didn't want my father to manage it. She gave it into the safe keeping of her – friend.

Jean And he did keep it.

Julie He did. My father finds this all out, but he can't take him to court, he can't pay his wife's lover back, and he can't prove that it is his wife's money. He wanted to shoot himself – they say he tried and failed. He recovered. He made my mother pay for what she had done. I loved my father, but I sided with my mother. I didn't know the ins and outs of it all. I've learned from her to hate men – she hated all men, you've heard that – I swore to her I would not be a slave to any man.

Jean Then you got yourself engaged to the County Attorney.

Julie So that he would become my slave.

Jean Did he not want to?

Julie He wanted to, but I wouldn't let him. I grew bored of him.

Jean I saw it – in the stableyard.

Julie What did you see?

Jean What I saw. He broke off the engagement.

Julie Lie. I did that. Has he claimed he did, the good-for-nothing?

Jean He's not that, I think. Miss Julie, you hate men.

Julie Yes. Always – almost. I get weak – then – Christ –

Jean You hate me as well?

Julie I hate you. I would like to put you down like an animal –

Jean Have the animal put down, and those who abused it get two years' hard labour, isn't that the law?

Julie It is.

Jean That law doesn't apply. No animals here. What are we going to do?

Julie Get away from here.

Jean And torment each other to death?

Julie No. Two days to love – eight days – as long as you can love – and then – die.

Jean Die? Ridiculous. It's better to open a hotel.

She is not listening to him.

Julie By Lake Como. The sun shines there all the time. The laurels are green at Christmas, and the oranges burn red –

Jean It pisses rain on Lake Como. The only oranges I saw were on fruit stalls. But it's a nice trap for tourists. There's loads of villas there for happy couples to rent. There's big profit in that. Do you know why? They lease for six months – and they leave after three weeks.

She asks naively:

Julie Three weeks? Why?

Jean They fight. But the rent still has to be paid. Then they lease it out again. That's the way it happens. There's plenty of love – even if it doesn't last too long.

Julie You don't want to die with me?

Jean I don't want to die at all. I enjoy my life, and I think suicide is sinful, it's against God who gave us life.

Julie You believe in God?

Jean Naturally I do, yes. I go to church every second Sunday. Look, I'm really tired of this – I'm off to bed.

Julie I see – you believe I can be tossed aside like that? Do you know when a man shames a woman he owes her a debt?

Jean takes out his wallet and throws a silver coin on the table.

Jean There you go. I wouldn't be in debt to anyone.

Miss Julie pretends not to have noticed the insult.

Julie Do you know what the law says –

Jean It's sad the law doesn't say when a woman's seduced a man, how she should be punished.

Julie Do you see any other escape – we go away, get married and then separate.

Jean And if I do not want to be part of this damaging marriage?

Julie Damaging?

Jean Most definitely. You see I come from a much better background than you do. None of my ancestors indulged in arson.

Julie You're sure of that?

Jean You can't contradict it – nobody recorded my family's history, apart from the parish. I've looked up your breeding in a book on the drawing-room table. Do you know who started your noble line? He was a miller. During the war with Denmark he let the king screw his wife. I can't boast such ancestors. I don't have a single ancestor, but I can become one myself.

Julie This is what I get for giving my heart to a dog – for dishonouring my family –

Jean Dishonour – yes, well, I told you so. You shouldn't drink because then you start talking. And really one should not talk.

Julie I do regret it – I really do. If you loved me at least –

Jean For the last time – what are you talking about? Do you want me to weep? Will I leap over your riding whip? Will I kiss you? Trick you into running away to Lake Como, stay with you for three weeks and then – what will I do then? What will you do? This is beginning to pain me. That's what happens when a man interferes in women's business. Miss Julie, I see the misery you're in. I know you're suffering, but I do not understand you. We're not like you. We don't have your sort of hatred. Love's like a game to us. When we've time off work, we play, but we don't have all night and day like you do! I think you're a sick woman, and your mother was seriously mad. Whole parishes about here have been affected by her kind of madness.

Julie Be gentle with me – you're talking to me now like a human being.

Jean You act like a human being as well. You spit on me, yet you won't let me wipe the spit dry – on you.

Julie Just help me, will you? What way should I go?

Jean In Christ's name, I wish I knew myself.

Julie Crazy – I've been insane – but there must surely be some way of saving myself.

Jean Calm – just be calm. Nobody knows a thing.

Julie That's not possible. Those people know – Kristin knows.

Jean They don't imagine anything like this happening – they couldn't.

She hesitates.

Julie But it could happen again.

Jean True.

Julie And what will they do?

Jean What will they do – I didn't think of that, have I taken leave of my senses? There's only one thing to do – get away. Now. You have to go on your own – everything's lost if I'm seen to follow you. Just get away – anywhere –

Julie Anywhere – on my own – I can't –

Jean You must. Before the Count comes back. We know what's going to happen if you stay. The harm's done. If you fall once, you fall again – you get to care less and less. That way you're found out. Just leave. Write to the Count later on. Tell him everything. But don't mention my name. He'll never ever guess that. And I don't imagine he would be too keen to know.

Julie Come with me and I'll go.

Jean Woman, are you a lunatic? Miss Julie runs off with her servant. It would be read in every newspaper the day after tomorrow. The Count could not survive that.

Julie How do I leave? How do I stay? Help me. I am worn out – my very bones are aching. Order me what to do. Force me to do something – I can't think anything, I can't do anything.

Jean Do you see now what you're cut from? Why do you give yourself such airs and walk the earth as if you owned it? All right, I'll order you. Get upstairs – get dressed. Get money together for the journey – then get downstairs.

She asks half-audibly:

Julie Come upstairs with me.

Jean To your bedroom? You're off your head again – (*He hesitates a moment.*) No – get out – now.

He takes her hand and leads her offstage.
She asks as she exits:

Julie Jean, speak kindly to me.

Jean You don't give orders of kindness, you bark them. Now you know what it feels like.

On his own, Jean heaves a sigh of relief.
He sits down by the table and takes out a notebook and pencil. He calculates something out loud.
This continues in dumb mime until Kristin enters dressed for church.
She holds a shirtfront and a white tie in her hand.

Kristin I've slept like a log.

Jean Dressed for church already, are you?

Kristin I am. What about yourself? You promised to come to communion with me today.

Jean I did, true enough. I see you've got my Sunday best. Come on then.

He sits down.
Kristin starts to dress him in the shirtfront and white tie.
There is a pause.
He asks sleepily:

Jean What's the reading for today?

Kristin John the Baptist getting his head chopped off.

Jean That one goes on and on. Watch, you're hanging me. I could sleep for a month, I really could.

Kristin Well, what has the big man been doing up all night? Look at the green face on him.

Jean I've been stuck here talking to Miss Julie.

Kristin That lady does not know the meaning of modesty.

There is a pause.

Jean Kristin?

Kristin What?

Jean Isn't it peculiar when you think of it – her –

Kristin What's peculiar?

Jean Everything.

There is a pause.
Kristin looks at the half-empty glasses standing on the table.

Kristin Have you been boozing together as well?

Jean We have.

Kristin To hell with you – it's not possible – is it?

He considers this briefly.

Jean Yes – it is.

Kristin I don't believe it – I can't, no – oh God –

Jean You're not jealous of her, are you?

Kristin Not of her – no. Klara or Sofi – either of them – I would have had your eyes. That's the way it is. Why – I don't know. But it's a dirty act.

Jean Are you in a rage against her?

Kristin A rage against you. That was a rotten thing to do – really rotten. Foolish girl. I'll tell you one thing.

46

I won't stay any longer in this house when I can no longer look up to my betters.

Jean Why do you have to look up to them?

Kristin The smart boy here can explain that to me. Do you want to dance attendance on people who have no decency? Do you? We'll all be tarred with the same brush, I say.

Jean Yes, but it's comforting for us to know they're not a bit better.

Kristin I take no comfort from it. If they are the dregs, there's not much point in us trying to improve ourselves. Think of the Count. Think of the suffering that man's endured in his day. Good Jesus. I will stay no longer in this house. And she did it with the likes of this boy. If it had been the County Attorney – if it had been someone from her own class –

Jean What then?

Kristin Well, you're no better nor worse than you should be, but there are distinctions between people. No, I cannot get over this. Miss Julie so haughty, so hard on all men – who would believe she'd throw herself at any man – especially a man like this. She's the one who insisted the bitch should be put down because she ran after the gamekeeper's dog. I'm saying it out straight. I'll stay here no longer. Come the twenty-fourth of October, I'll be gone.

Jean What then?

Kristin Then you might start looking for work seeing that we're supposed to get married. That's what then.

Jean So what should I look for? When I'm a married man I can't get a position like this.

Kristin No, you can't. You'll have to look for a job as a caretaker or a porter in a government office. The money at the Civil Service is bad, but it's a safe job with a pension for the wife and children –

He grimaces.

Jean Is that so? I don't intend to die just yet for my wife and children. I must admit my ambitions were slightly higher.

Kristin Oh, you have ambitions, do you? You have obligations as well. You might think of them.

Jean Don't preach to me about obligations. I know what I've got to do. (*He listens to what's happening offstage.*) We'll have time enough to think about that. Get yourself ready, we'll head off to church.

Kristin Who's that wandering about upstairs?

Jean Maybe it's Klara.

Kristin It wouldn't be the Count – he wouldn't have come home and no one's heard him?

Jean is frightened.

Jean The Count? No – that's not true – he would have rang for me – I know that.

Kristin exits.

Kristin God, look down on us. I've never found myself in the likes of this before.

The sun rises.
  It lights the tops of the trees in the park.
  The light moves slowly until it falls in a slant through the windows.
  Jean goes over to the door and gives Miss Julie a sign.

Miss Julie enters dressed in travelling clothes.
She carries a small birdcage, covered with a towel.
She places it on a chair.

Julie I'm ready now.

Jean Hold your tongue. Kristin is awake.

Miss Julie is growing increasingly nervous.

Julie Does she suspect anything?

Jean Nothing – she knows nothing. Christ, the look of
you.

Julie What? How do I look?

Jean You're as pale as a ghost. I'm sorry to say this –
your face is filthy.

Julie Let me clean it then. (*She goes to the washing bowl
and cleans her face and hands.*) Give me a towel. Look –
the sun's rising.

Jean Then the demons' work is done.

Julie They were busy last night. Jean, listen to me. Come
with me. I have the money now.

He hesitates.

Jean Enough money?

Julie Enough to make a start. Come with me – I can't
travel alone today. It's Midsummer. Imagine being stuck
on that train, surrounded by people. Every eye would be
fixed on me. I wouldn't be able to breathe. We would
have to stop at every train station when what we want
to do is fly, fly. No. I can't, I can't. The memories would
start. I'd remember when I was a child – the church on
Midsummer Day was thick with leaves and branches.
Birch twigs and lilacs. We'd feast at the happy table,
friends, relations – and the afternoon in the garden,

dancing, music, flowers, playing games. You can run away for the rest of your life, but the memories, they weigh you down like your luggage. They bring you remorse, they hurt your conscience.

Jean I will go with you. It has to be now before it's too late. I mean now, this minute.

Julie Get dressed then. (*She takes the bird-cage.*)

Jean Take no luggage. That will give the game away.

Julie Nothing, no. Only what we can carry and ourselves.

Jean has taken his hat.

Jean What's that – what have you there?

Julie My greenfinch – that's all. I can't leave it behind.

Jean Is that so – we're bringing a bird-cage, are we? You are off your head. Let it go.

Julie This is all I'm taking from my own home. The one living creature that cares for me since Diana betrayed me. Don't be cruel. Let me keep it.

Jean I'm saying, let it go. Keep your voice down. Kristin will hear us.

Julie I'm not handing it to strangers – I'd rather kill it.

Jean Give me the bastard and I'll wring its neck.

Julie All right, but don't let it suffer, don't – I can't, no –

Jean Give me it – I can do it.

She takes the bird from the cage and kisses it.

Julie My tiny Serine, are you going to die and leave Mama?

Jean Please, no scenes. We're talking about your life, your survival. Come on, quickly.

*He takes the bird from her, goes to the chopping
board and takes the kitchen axe.*
  Miss Julie turns away.

Jean You wasted your time learning to shoot with a gun.
Better for you to behead a few chickens. (*He chops.*) You
might not faint then at the sight of a drop of blood.

She screams.

Julie Take my life as well – take it. That creature is
innocent. You can kill it and your hands don't shake.
I despise – I hate you. There is blood between us. I curse
the day I set eyes on you, I curse the day I was conceived
in my mother's womb.

Jean Your curses won't help you. Get a move on.

*She approaches the chopping board as if drawn
against her will.*

Julie No – not yet – I don't want to – I can't – I need to
see – ssh, there's a carriage coming up the road – (*She
listens, her eyes firmly fixed all the while on the chopping
board and axe.*) I can't stomach the sight of blood –
that's what you think – I'm weak – am I – I'd like to see
your blood, your brains smashed on the chopping block.
I want to see every one of your sex swimming in a lake
of blood like this one. I think I could drink out of your
skull – I could wash my feet in your ripped stomach –
I could roast your heart and eat. So you think I am
weak. You think I love you – and blessed be your seed
in my womb. You think I'll carry your child beneath my
heart and my blood will nourish it – I'll give you a child
and I'll take your name. Tell me, what is your name? I've
never heard your surname. Have you got one? I don't
suppose you do. So I'll become Mrs Doorman – or
maybe Mrs Shitspreader – you are a dog who wears my
collar – you are the son of a labourer – you wear my

coat of arms on your buttons. I have to share you with my cook. I am my servant's rival. Dear sweet God! You think I'm a coward who wants to run away. No, I'll stay now. What will be, will be. My father will return home. He'll find his desk broke open. His money vanished. He'll ring then – on that bell there. Ring twice for his lackey. He'll send for the police. And I will tell him everything. Everything. It will be wonderful to put an end to this – if only that could be the end. His heart will break. He will die. That will be the end for each and every one of us. Quiet – we will all be at peace – eternal rest – they break the coat of arms over the coffin – the Count's line has ended. The lackey's child survives in an orphanage – he will win the praise of the gutter and end up behind bars.

Jean Listen to the spouting of the royal blood. Well done, Miss Julie. Bury the miller in his sack.

Kristin enters, dressed for church, with a hymn-book in her hand. Miss Julie rushes towards her.
She falls into her arms, as if seeking protection.

Julie Kristin, help me. Save me from this man.

Kristin is unmoved and cold.

Kristin What sort of racket are you making on a Sunday morning? (*She notices the chopping board.*) Look at the state of that. What are you doing? Why are you roaring and screaming like this?

Julie You're a woman, Kristin, and you're my friend. Take care against that good-for-nothing.

Jean is disconcerted.

Jean The ladies are engaged in conversation, so I'll go and shave.

He slips out stage right.

Julie You have to understand me – you have to listen –

Kristin I do not understand this carry on. Where is my lady going dressed in travelling clothes? Why is Jean wearing a hat? Why is that?

Julie Kristin, listen to me, I'll tell you everything, listen –

Kristin I want to know nothing –

Julie Listen – you have to listen –

Kristin About what? This silly nonsense with Jean, is that it? I do not care in the slightest. But if you think you'll trick him into eloping with you, I can put a sure stop to your gallop.

Miss Julie is even more nervous.

Julie Please be calm, Kristin, and listen to me. I can't stay here – Jean can't stay here – we have to get away

Kristin eyes her and Miss Julie brightens up.

Julie So I've had this idea, you see. The three of us go together – go abroad – Switzerland. We start a hotel together – I've money, you see – Jean and I, we'd take care of everything. And I thought that you would take charge of the kitchen. Wouldn't that be lovely? Say yes, please. Come away with us – then everything will be settled. Say yes, do, please.

She embraces Kristin and pats her back.
Kristin eyes her coldly and thoughtfully.
Miss Julie speaks at great speed.

Julie Kristin, you've never travelled. Get out and see the world – do. Such fun to travel by train. New people constantly – new places – we'll visit the zoo in Hamburg – you'll like that – the theatre and the opera – in Munich we'll get to the museum – Rubens, Raphael, great painters you know – you have heard about Munich –

where King Ludwig lived – the king who went mad, you know – we'll see his castle – exactly like in fairy tales and it's not far from there to Switzerland – the Alps, you know – the Alps – imagine – snow on top in the middle of the summer – oranges grow there and laurels green all year round.

Jean can be seen in the wings sharpening his razor on a strap which he holds with his teeth and left hand.
He listens to the conversation with a pleased expression, nodding approval in places. Miss Julie speaks with even greater speed than before.

Julie We'll open a hotel – I'll keep guard behind the counter and Jean will greet the guests – does the shopping – writes a letter – believe me, it's a fine life – the train whistles, the carriage arrives, the bell rings upstairs, it rings in the restaurant – I'll write the bills – I'll salt them, I will – you would not believe how paying bills scares the wits out of the guests – you – you will be in charge of the kitchen. You won't be standing over a stove – no – no – you'll be well-dressed because you'll be introduced to people – and I'm not flattering you – you'll land yourself a husband one fine day with your looks. You'll see – a grand English gentleman – these people are very easy to – (*She slows down.*) Land. We'll grow rich. Build ourselves a villa at Lake Como. It does rain there – sometimes it does rain – but – (*Her voice falters.*) The sun has to shine there once in a while – just when it's at its darkest – and – then – if it doesn't – we can go back home, can't we – and just go back – (*She pauses.*) Here – or some place else –

Kristin Stop this. Do you yourself believe any of it, Miss Julie?

Miss Julie is crushed.

Julie Do I believe it?

Kristin Yes.

Miss Julie is exhausted.

Julie I don't know. I don't believe in anything any more. (*She collapses on the bench and drops her head between her arms on the table.*) Nothing at all. Nothing.

Kristin turns to where Jean is standing.

Kristin So he was thinking of doing a runner.

Disconcerted, Jean puts the razor down on the table.

Jean A runner? That's putting it too harshly. You've heard what Miss Julie is proposing. She may be exhausted without her night's sleep but we can still carry out her proposal.

Kristin Listen to that. Was the intention that I would cook for that –

Jean interrupts sharply:

Jean Keep a decent tongue in your head when you're addressing your mistress. Do you hear?

Kristin Mistress?

Jean Yes.

Kristin Listen to that. Listen to him.

Jean Listen to you – listen more and talk less. Miss Julie is your mistress. You spit on her now but you might spit on yourself for the same reason.

Kristin I've always had enough respect for myself –

Jean Enough to spit on others –

Kristin Enough to never lower myself beneath my station. No man can say that the Count's cook threw herself at the stable-boy or the pig-keeper. No man can say that.

Jean Yes, you've been enjoying yourself with the right gentleman – that's been your good luck.

Kristin A right gentleman, yes – he steals oats from the Count's stables –

Jean You're a fine one to talk. You take your cut from the grocery money – you take bribes from the butcher.

Kristin What are you saying?

Jean And you, yes you, you can no longer respect your betters.

Kristin Are you coming to church? After your big talk you could do with a good sermon.

Jean I'm not going to church today, no. Go by yourself, fall on your knees and confess your sins.

Kristin I'll do that, yes. And I'll come home and forgive you as well. The Saviour suffered on the cross. He died for all our sins. If we come to him with faith, if we repent, he will take all our guilt on himself.

Jean Will he forgive those who stole food?

Julie Do you believe that, Kristin?

Kristin As sure as I'm alive, as I'm standing here, that is my faith. The faith of my childhood. I've stayed firm in it, Miss Julie. Where there is a multitude of sin, there is a multitude of grace.

Julie If I had your faith – if I –

Kristin You can't have it. It comes only through the grace of God and he does not grant it to everyone –

Julie So who does he grant it to?

Kristin The last shall be the first – that's the great mystery of grace, Miss Julie. God doesn't have favourites. The last –

Julie So he favours the last –

Kristin continues:

Kristin Shall be first, and it is easier for a camel to pass through the eye of a needle than for a rich man to enter the Kingdom of God. That's the way God planned it, Miss Julie. Well I'm going now – going on my own. I'll tell the stable boy when I'm leaving not to lend anybody any horses – someone might want to do a runner before the Count gets home. Farewell. (*She exits.*)

Jean There goes the devil. And all this because of a green-finch.

Miss Julie is numb.

Julie Leave the green-finch out of it. Do you see any ending – any way out of this?

Jean No.

Julie If you were in my place, what would you do?

Jean Me – in your place – wait a minute. If I were of noble blood – If I were a woman who – fell – I don't know. I do – I do know.

She has taken the razor and makes a gesture.

Julie This?

Jean Yes. But I wouldn't do it. Make a note of that. That's the difference between us.

Julie You're a man, and I am a woman – what difference is that?

Jean The same difference between a man and a woman.

Miss Julie has the razor in her hand.

Julie I want to. I can't. My father couldn't either, the time he should have.

Jean No, he shouldn't have. He needed his revenge first.

Julie And now through me, my mother gets her revenge.

Jean Have you never loved your father, Miss Julie?

Julie I love him with all my heart and soul, but I loathe him too. I did that without knowing it. He brought me up to hate my own sex. I am woman, and I am man. Who's to blame for what happened? My father? My mother? Myself? Is it myself? Have I nothing that is mine? Every thought I've had, I took from my father. Every passion I've felt came from my mother. And the last hope – everybody is equal – that I got from the man I was to marry, and for that reason I call him good-for-nothing. How can it be my own fault? Should I blame Jesus, like Kristin did – no, I won't do that. I think too much of myself, I know myself too well – thank you, Father, for teaching me that. A rich man can't enter the Kingdom of God – what a lie. Kristin has money saved in the bank – so she's barred for sure. Who's to blame? Who gives a curse who's to blame? In the end I will take the blame on my own two shoulders, and I will face the music.

Jean Yes, but –

The bell rings sharply twice.
Miss Julie leaps to her feet.
Jean changes his coat.

Jean The Count – he's home. What if Kristin – (*He goes to the speaking tube, taps it and listens.*)

Julie Has he been to his desk yet?

Jean listens.
The audience does not hear what the Count says.

Jean Yes, my Lord. (*He listens.*) At once, my Lord. (*He listens.*) In half an hour – yes.

She is even more distressed.

Julie What did he say? In the name of Jesus, what did he say?

Jean His boots – his coffee – he wants them in half an hour.

Julie Half an hour, I am worn out. I can do nothing. I can't say I'm sorry, can't run away, can't stay, I cannot live, I cannot die. Help me. Bark me an order and I'll obey like a dog. Save my honour, save my name – do me that one last favour. You know what I want to do. I can't. Force me to do it. Command me to do it.

Jean I can't – I don't know why either – I don't understand – I put on this coat and it makes me – I can't order you about – now since the Count spoke to me – I can't say what I mean – but – I will live and die a servant – if that man the master were to walk in and order me to cut my throat, I believe I would do it here and now.

Julie Pretend you're him, and I'm you. You acted so well when you were on your knees – then you had blue blood – or have you ever been to the theatre and seen a hypnotist –

Jean indicates he has.

Julie He says, take the broom, and you take it. He says, sweep, and you sweep.

Jean You have to be asleep first though –

Miss Julie is in ecstasy.

Julie I think I'm sleeping already. I think the whole room is filled with smoke. You look like an iron stove, and it looks like a man dressed in black, wearing a top hat, and your eyes, they're like coal glowing when the fire's dying, and your face is the colour of ashes.

The sun's rays stretch across the floor and lighten Jean.

Julie It's so warm – so very warm – (*She rubs her hands as if warming them before a fire.*) Full of light – peace –

Jean takes the razor and puts it in her hand.

Jean Here – go into the daylight – in to the barn – and –

He whispers in her ear.
She is awake now.

Julie Thank you. I can go to my rest now. Tell me this – the first and the last – can the first receive the gift of grace? Tell me, even if you don't believe it.

Jean The first? I can't, no. Miss Julie – wait. You're no longer among the first. You're standing among the last.

Julie I am among the last. I am the last. Still – I can't go now. Tell me again to go.

Jean I can't – I can't.

Julie And the last shall be the first.

Jean Stop thinking about it – stop. You're draining my strength, you're turning me into a coward. Look, I think I heard the bell – no. Will we put some paper round it? Frightened of a bell, so frightened. It's not just a bell – there is someone behind it – a hand makes it move – and something else makes the hand move – put your hands over your ears – put your hands over your ears – just do that. I will, and he'll ring louder. He'll keep ringing until you answer. It will be too late then. The police will be here – then –

The bell rings twice, forcefully.
Jean startles, then straightens up.

Savage – there is no other way out – go.

Miss Julie exits through the door with complete determination.

THE STRONGER

For Mike and Joan and Cash

The Stronger was first produced by Project Arts Centre in Bewley's Café, Grafton Street, Dublin, in 1993, with the following cast:

Mme X Joan Sheehy
Mlle Y Bairbre Ní Caoimh
Waitress Tara Quirke

Directed by Judy Friel

Characters

Mme X
Mlle Y
A Waitress

The corner of a fashionable café.
  Two iron tables, expensive chairs.
  Madame X enters, dressed for winter, a Japanese
basket in her arms.
  Mademoiselle Y sits reading illustrated magazines,
a glass of wine in front of her.

Mme X No, it's herself. Herself alone. And on a Christmas Eve. Imagine you being here alone, like an old man without wife or children. Amelia.

  Mlle Y looks up, nods, goes back to reading.

I'm mortified to see you like this, I am. On Christmas Eve, alone, all on your ownio on the day that's in it. Where was it I saw that wedding? Yes, in Paris, when I was there – it was quite a fancy restaurant, and I remember it because the bride was sitting alone reading a child's comic and the groom, he was playing poker with the best man. It took my breath away. I said to myself, well, what chance do these two have in a marriage if this is how they begin it? How will it end, yes? Playing cards on his wedding day, the happiest day of anybody's life. So what, you're going to say, she was reading a comic? But it's not – it's not – you know yourself.

  A Waitress enters, placing a cup of chocolate in front of Mme X, exits.

Amelia? You should have held onto him. I do sincerely think that. Do you remember, wasn't it my good self who said the same to you. Forgive, forgive. Do you remember? If you'd only have listened to me, you could be happily hitched by now, with a lovely home of your own. Remember last Christmas? Who was the happy woman to be taken to meet his parents down in the country? What was it you said? 'A happy home life, that's what I want. To hell with the theatre, I'm getting out of it.' Your very words. My poor child – 'a happy home life' – that's the making of us. The theatre, aah! And children, your own children, you know yourself – no, you don't, do you? Forgive, forgive.

Mlle Y looks at her in disgust.
Mme X sips her chocolate, opens her basket and takes out her presents.

These are for my brood. See what I've got for them. (*She takes out a doll.*) Look at this, look. It's for Lisa. Look at her, making eyes and the way her head moves. Yes. And this little fellow is for Maja.

She loads the toy pistol and fires the cork on its string at Mlle Y, who starts in fear.

What? What? Did I scare you? You thought I wanted to shoot you? Didn't you? Yes? What are you thinking, girl? I could well believe you wanted to shoot me – I did cross your path and I know, I know you can't forget and forgive, but you should know by now it honestly wasn't my fault. I did not get the theatre to replace you. I didn't, no matter what you think. And you think I was responsible. Well, no point wasting breath arguing. You won't hear me. (*She takes out a pair of embroidered slippers.*) For my love, my husband. See, the tulips. I embroidered them with my own fair hand. Tulips, I detest them. He'd have them stitched everywhere.

Mlle Y looks up from her magazine, registering a cynical interest.
Mme X puts a hand into each slipper.

70

Hasn't he got such tiny feet? Yes, hasn't he? And the way he walks, so like a dancer, yes? But then you've never seen him wearing slippers.

Mlle Y laughs out loud.

Will I show you how he walks? (*She walks the slippers about the table.*)

Mlle Y laughs out loud again.

But my dear, when he gets cross, he stamps his foot, just like this. 'Damn, damn, damn, does no one in this house know how to make a cup of coffee? Lord God, what idiot left the lights in here blazing?' And say there's a bit of a breeze blowing under the door and his feet are cold, it's, 'Is there nobody in this house capable of lighting a fire?' (*She rubs the sole of a slipper against the top of the other one.*)

Mlle Y bursts out laughing.

When home is the hero and he can't find his slippers – little Majy's hidden them under the sideboard – well, the shouts – . No. No, it's evil to make a mockery of my husband, the man is a dote. A complete dote. The kind of man you should have hooked, Amelia. You're laughing, why? Why? Yes? He's honest with me, he is. Loyal, he is. I know, faithful. I do. He told me – you're smiling, why the smile? – he himself told me that Fran, that bitch, she made a pass at him. Can you believe the neck of her?

Silence.

If she walked through my door, I would blind her.

Silence.

Thank God I heard it all from his own lips. Imagine hearing it through gossip.

71

Silence

She wasn't the only whore. I know. What is it about my lover boy, why do women throw themselves at him? Why? Do they think he can put in a good word for them at the theatre because he has the ear of you know who? Do they think he would do that for them? Do you? Do you? You, I'm never completely certain about you, I don't know. I do know he hasn't a passing interest in you. None. I know that. I also think you wish him ill. I always have.

Silence.
They look carefully at each other.

Amelia? Come and eat with us tonight. Show you're not in pain because of us, because of me at any rate, yes? I detest falling out with old friends. Falling out with you, it's not right. Is it because I crossed your path that time and – (*Her speech slows.*) I – just – don't – have – a – clue –

Silence.
Mlle Y looks enquiringly at Mme X.

When I met you, I was frightened of you. It's funny that we became friends. I watched you like a hawk, that's how terrified I was. No matter where I went, I had you stuck to my side. I called you my friend to stop you becoming my enemy. When you came to our house, I panicked. I could see my husband loathed you. I felt – not comfortable, as if the clothes I was wearing weren't my own size or shape. I bent over backwards to get him to be kind to you, but he wouldn't be. Then you go off and get engaged, and you and my husband suddenly become great pals – why? Were you frightened too? Frightened to show what you really felt when you were – available? So. So, what happened next? Does it seem strange I wasn't jealous? I wasn't. Remember my first –

our first child, the christening? I asked you to be godmother. I told him, I let him kiss you. That distressed you, it did, though I didn't take heed of it then – it hasn't crossed my mind – hasn't entered my head until – this precise moment. (*She rises suddenly.*) Why are you silent? You've not spoken. Since I came in here, not a word out of you. You sit there, you let me babble on, you're staring at me, you worm all these bits and pieces out of me. You're winding me round your finger like a silken thread. You're enjoying all my doubts, aren't you? Why? Can I guess? Why did you call off your engagement? You never set foot inside our house after that – why? Why won't you eat with us tonight?

Mlle Y is about to speak.

No. Say nothing. There's no need. I see all now. *I* know why – why you – why you – *you*. Yes, I see. It makes sense now. That's it. Damn you, why am I sitting at the same table as you? (*She moves her things to another table.*) Tulips, you like tulips, and I detest them, so I must embroider them on his slippers because you – you – yes, I know. (*She throws the slippers to the ground.*) Now I know why we had to spend that last stifling summer so far from the sea. You detest the sea. I know why my son Edward – my son has your father, Edward's name. I know why I wear your favourite colours, read what you like to read, eat what you eat, drink what you drink – this may as well be your cup of chocolate. I know, I know – hard, hard. Everything you wanted you got through me. Everything. You have eaten me skin and bone. You have peeled my soul like an apple and left it to rot. I wanted to get away from you, I couldn't. You still me with your witch's eyes, you pin me down, you spit your serpent's poison at me. If I had wings, you'd slice them from me. If I went to the water, you'd tie my feet and let me drown. If I tried to swim, I'd sink deeper and deeper down until I reached rock bottom. That's where you're lying in wait for me, I can feel your crab's claws. You're waiting for me. You. I hate you. I do hate you. Hate. Sitting there, not one word out of you. Silent. Sedate. Selfish. Do you notice if it's day or night? Do you feel if it's winter or summer? Do you hear if people laugh or cry? You don't because you cannot hate and you cannot love. You are a worn out woman. You can't catch a man. You can't win a man. You have to lie in wait for him. You sit stuck in your rat hole. That's what your corner's called, do you know that? Look at you. You scavenge your way through newspaper stories feeding on whoever is in bother, on whoever is dying, on whoever's been kicked out of a play. Look at you, living for the bad word, looking out for the boat that's sinking and waving to whoever's dragged down with it, waiting for the dead to drop in front of you, always waiting, waiting. You've been destroyed and you're evil because you're destroyed. Poor woman. Sad, sad woman. Amelia. Amelia. Evil, sad. I'm sorry for you. How can I be angry with you, even if I wanted to be. You can't help it. You're a lost child. Weak, weak as a baby. Your little fling with my husband? It doesn't take a wrinkle out of me. And if it was you taught me to like drinking chocolate? So what? Someone else would have anyway. Who cares? (*She sips the chocolate and continues confidently.*) Chocolate is supposed to be good for a body, yes? And so I dress as you do? Good, so be it. *Voilà.* It made my husband love me all the more. Too bad for you, all the better for me. And if I can put two and two together, I'd guess you've lost him. Did you hope I'd fade away? You're the one that's fading – and now here you've landed, lamenting it ever happened. Me, I've no regrets. No point crowing. Who'd want something no one else puts a value on? Who knows, maybe, when push comes to shove, between the two of us, I'm the stronger. Maybe, at this precise moment. You never got anything from me. You gave and you gave. Do you remember believing in fairy tales? The wicked thief? You fell into your beauty sleep, but I got away with the gold. When you touch anything, it falls apart for you. It breaks. It's barren. All your tulips, all your traumas, they can't keep a man in your arms. And I have kept mine. You never learned about this life from all your books, and I did learn. You had a father who had a name, but I have a son with a father, and with your father's name. You're still being very quiet, aren't you? Quiet, quiet. Why? One time I believed it so because you were strong. Maybe you just had nothing to offer. For you don't have a brain in your body. (*She gets up, taking the slippers.*) Tulips, your tulips, I'll take them home with me. You couldn't hear what people were saying, you looked and didn't learn. I did. You're dry as dust. You'll break down and blow away. Thank you, teacher. Thank you, mistress. You've been good to me, Amelia. Thank you, you taught my husband how to love. I'm going home to him now, to love. (*She goes.*)

CPSIA information can be obtained at www.ICGtesting.com
Printed in the USA
LVOW11s0255051016

507463LV00001B/3/P